THE
PHOENIX
TRINITY

Matthew Gregory Rowbatham

NEWMAN SPRINGS PUBLISHING
320 Broad Street
Red Bank, NJ 07701

First originally published by Newman Springs Publishing 2020

ISBN 978-1-64801-238-9 (Paperback)
ISBN 978-1-64801-239-6 (Digital)

Printed in the United States of America

To the Little Sunflower on my rainy days.
                                    Love, Matthew

CONTENTS

PROLOGUE

My Mind

A Maze

My mind,
a maze.
Constantly changing,
and rearranging.

One day the way out is easily found,
and the next it's nearly impossible to solve.

See those days are the worst
My thoughts are cloudy,
like trying to see through a fog.
My emotions are overlapping,
like a last minute collage project.

Never knowing how I feel,
just knowing I wish I couldn't anymore;

Wish I couldn't feel happy
Wish I couldn't feel sad
Wish I couldn't feel love
Wish I couldn't feel hate
Wish I couldn't feel anything

Because on those days I feel everything,
it's something you never get used to.

Feeling happy and sad at the same time,
it's like being split in two,
but never fully torn apart.
Constantly tortured by the pain,
until the day comes,

When the maze is easily solved,
and the pain is forgotten for a moment.

When that day comes,
Healed by the love you share,
and the emotions you feel.
It feels like your life's on cruise control
Time flying by, with an open mind.

It's something you never get used to
feeling everything.

Feeling happy!
Feeling sad!
Feeling love!
Feeling hate!
Feeling everything!

Knowing how I feel,
and accepting it with open arms.

Like lying in an open field,
my thoughts are clear.
Like two dance partners,
my emotions are paired.
See those days are the best.

Then the next day the maze is impossible to solve,
Until one day it's easily found.

Rearranging, and
changing constantly.
The maze,
in my head.

A Prison

My mind,
a prison,
for my emotions,
that's the notion.

"Emotions? Lock them away.
Make yourself numb to the pain."
That's what I used to say,
to keep them at bay.

Bang! Pow!
Emotions all around.

Duck! Dodge!
They knock me to the ground.

Scream! Shout!
Because I can't let them out.

A Ballroom

My mind,
a ballroom,
beautiful chaos,
moving to the beat.

A slow song,
like moving in water.
Precise with every movement.
Locking eyes with…who?
A friend?
A loved one?
A lover?
I can't tell,
but the emotions are strong,
endearing, filled with love.

A fast song,
like flying through the sky.
Limbs owned by the beat.
Mind empty, my body is in control now.
What song is this?
Who am I dancing with?
Where am I?
Not relevant,
but the emotions are strong,
joyful, filled with cheer!

PART 1

DECAY

Faceless

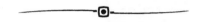

My only friend?
The only thing I let in?
Faceless feelings formed this figure
and now I'm in danger

At first it was nice,
he made me feel...
alright?
But then things changed.

I made him mad.
I let someone else in.
He didn't like that,
and he's making me pay him back!

Emotions turned black,
heartless now,
a rage filled void
inside my head.

I can't let go,
I still need him!

He's me,
and I am him!

Now he's in control,
and I can't turn him back!

Dying

You can't see the point of all this self diminish.
You feel like you don't exist; you're unfinished.
You think you might be dying.
From all the meds that you've been taking.
(1)
From all the pain and sorrow you're feeling.
(2)
From all your demons, you think you're drowning.
(3)

---

1. To keep yourself from the killer
2. That close you off; that hinder
3. In all their blood, you're in a thriller
4. From all the hate that you've received
5. Every time you've been deceived
6. Found in the people you've believed

Living

You need a new life 'cause yours ain't worth any.
Not time, love, or even a penny.
But, you keep living.
To feel the love that pain starts bringing.
(4)
To heal the wounds that you've been digging.
(5)
To find the love and strength worth fighting.
(6)

---

1. To keep yourself from the killer
2. That close you off; that hinder
3. In all their blood, you're in a thriller
4. From all the hate that you've received
5. Every time you've been deceived
6. Found in the people you've believed

Trapping yourself

Trapping yourself
(1)
Behind the doors
(2)
Of the battlefield
(3)
Fuels the fire,
(4)
Feeds the beast,
(5)
And blinds your love,
(6)
Trapping yourself

---

1. To keep yourself from the killer

2. That close you off; that hinder

3. In all their blood, you're in a thriller

4. From all the hate that you've received

5. Every time you've been deceived

6. Found in the people you've believed

Empty Dreaming

Empty dreaming,
floating through my feelings,
fighting all the demons left.

Feeling like I'm leaning,
started heavy breathing,
now my head screams, Help!

Feeling like I'm running out of space…
Fighting each and every single day…
To cure myself and start to pave my way…

Empty dreaming!
Darkness breathing!
No feelings are left!

I'm crying and I'm bleeding!
My demons, they are winning!
Body turns to dust…

A***

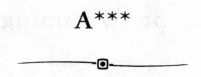

You count the sheep,
you can not sleep.
The heat of battle,
the fear and fright.
All in your head,
that's what they said

A Room With No Friends

Lying in bed, but not for sleep.
A place for thoughts to retreat.
Alone with no more hate,
where no one can discriminate.
                    A room with no "friends".
A place where emotions are accepted,
and feelings are expected.
Because here is your own retreat,
a place for you to release.
                    A room with no "friends".
Crying if that's what it takes
to express yourself; to escape,
from the demons you disguise
under your face; fake.
                    A room with no "friends".
Fake, are those who call you "friend"
then turn their backs.
That shout your "name" but say it wrong
with bad intent.
Fake is living your life happily,
when happiness has long been left.
                    A room with no "friends".
Left with the love, and the truth.
Left in the wake of this destructive wave
of emotions that you hide
behind your mask; Fake.
Until you enter the room,
The room, alone, with finally no more friends.

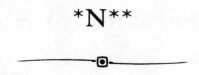

*N**

Perfectionist at your best,
but trapped in your curse's crest.
An ever changing maze
your subconscious has made.
To tie you down,
to pain.

Walking through the rain

Walking through the rain
Drowning out that distant pain
Staring at you through a windowpane
Lock it up; Contain

Walking through the rain
Wet with tears, washing down the drain
Gripping tight to what is sane
Drenched in fear; Afraid

Walking through the rain
Not a friendly face, but…pain
Demons screaming in your brain
Faceless voices; Insane

Walking through the rain
The voices, they fill your veins
Keep them locked up far away
Tie them down; Restrain

Walking through the rain
They're breaking free of the chain
They're latching on to all that pain
Screaming at you; Ordain

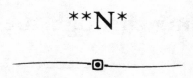

N

You can't explain, it's like you're locked in your own brain.
You can't find the key (not like there was one in the first place), that will set you free.
You see a kite, is it a lost memory? A distant thought?
You wanna chase it but then you question, "Is it safe?"
You sit back down, on the cold hard ground, with only your thoughts.
"Is anything safe?"

Feelings

I'm lost in my feelings

I feel it

The pain and the hate

I conceal it

To hide in myself

I can't believe it

I've lost all control

I can see it

The moments are gone

They're fleeting

Lost in this time

No more feeling

Too much self-containment

Now I'm screaming!

Waste of Tears

Waste of tears,
lost in fear,
depression, will it heal?

Thoughts unclear,
can no longer hear,
the voices are trying to make a deal.

Crawl down here,
your demon's near,
Don't let it break the seal!

"Help ME!"
"Free my soul!"
"I need someone to know!"

Water dripping, tears,
can they hear?
Echoes thrown, are they clear?

Ripped In Two

Stabbed into
Torn apart
Ripped in two

You're worthless! Emotions weak like glass! Broken with little force, shattered if rattled worse!	Help me... I've trapped myself. It's so, dark. I can't get out!
Pick it up! Don't cut yourself! It'll only make it worse! Shards, need to be put back together.	Left alone, an empty home. Emotions, I let them take control. Help?
Look at you! So miserable! No wonder no one loves YOU! Broken, battered, beaten!	Please calm them down. (NOW!) I'm gown to drown. Swimming in my tears. My end is near.

Pain

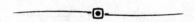

There's darkness in my brain!
My emotions they restrain!
I'm shackled and I'm chained!
I'm numb to all this pain!
You don't know anything!
There's demons, I'm insane!
They're screaming out my name!
Now I'm writing down my pain!

Call it scripture, not a saint.
'Cause I'm yelling out in vain!
Hoping one day I'll be…sane?

Fear

Hide
Scream
Run to bed
Not knowing if this will ever end

Yell
Cower
Close your eyes
Not knowing where evil truly lies

Tears
Cries
A heavy chain
Not knowing how to numb the pain

Love
Death
Two as one
Not knowing if you have ever won

Lie
Truth
Speak their name
Not knowing which one is to blame

***A

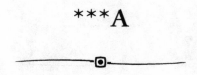

The only ones who see
are the ones in need
just like me
The only ones who see
are the ones in need
just like me

They Said

"Go to college."

That's what they said, and that was intent
but stress pressed you thin
and depression crawled on in.
Now you're trapped in your own skin
fighting battles you'll "never" win.

> Hoping to find a way to cure yourself, to ease the pain
> Praying for the day you clear the way, and stop the rain

And they don't listen.
The tears on your face, they glisten,
from all the pain and friction,
but still they don't see them, they don't listen.
Your dreams to them just seem like fiction.

> Hoping to find a way to cure yourself, to ease the pain
> Praying for the day you clear the way, and stop the rain

A year passes, unlike your classes.
You tried your best, with no success.
Afraid to let them know, or share your crown,
because you never wanted to let them down,
you never wanted to see them frown.

Hoping to find a way to cure yourself, to ease the pain
Praying for the day you clear the way, and stop the rain

So yes there was no "winning",
because you thought losing
would keep them grinning.
Until now. Now you are fighting,
coming back; reviving.

Leave this Earth

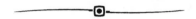

"Hell's a long way from Earth,
you don't want to jump first.
Before knowing your true worth,
because you can take far worse."

That's what they said.

But could you hear?
The voices, oh so sheer.

They spoke the truth,
and you let them lose

You could hear them
I know you could,

but you decided to ignore.
You decided that there was no point.

No point in hearing them,
because you thought it was too late.

Too late to fix your mistake.
Too late to clean up the messes you made.

Well now you are in a world where
the love you used to know has turned to hate.

Where so many people have fallin' in your wake,
because you were too selfish, too full of hate.

You broke them down,
you shared your crown,

but your kingdom was not wanted.
It was full of so much destruction

the alleys echoed with pain,
the streets filled with rain.

Not rain, but…tears, filled with fear.
Washing away the joy that once existed,

leaving behind the hate that twisted
your life, that is no longer rife.

This is what you left behind,
your legacy, and it's far from divine.

If only you listened,
To the loved ones that had you christened.

Now this is what they say.

"Why'd you have to go,
you left and I don't know…
how long I can go
without you. Why'd you go?"

"Why'd you leave this earth
gone for good, the reverse of birth.
It's a long way to Hell,
you didn't even wait for the bell."

"You tapped out before the end,
and made it hard to watch for your friend.
Why'd you go?
Why...?"

The Devil's Prey

Lost within a never ending maze,
setting your thoughts ablaze.
Your demon cannot be contained
He's broken free of his chains,
and now he's calling out your name.

> Battles fought at every turn
> A mental war zone set to burn

You're growing weak,
you won't last much longer.
He's wearing you down,
waiting for you to give in.
Will you wear his crown?

> You're fighting back against his sin.
> Will you let him in? Will you let him win?

You call for help,
you scream and yell,
but no one hears.
No one sees,
all the pain you bear.

> He's chipped away, your walls are thin.
> You're breaking down, and he's coming in.

The war is over,
but you didn't clear the maze.
and he's planted his seed.
Stress and hate is all it needs
for the depression to bloom.

The person you used to be,
now locked away without a key.

You've become numb to the pain,
and let go of what kept you sane.
A slave shackled and chained.
A zombie to the ideas he laid.
Locked up and left astray.

All you want is to be set loose,
but you don't know how to tie a noose

Reminder

Mental scars remind us,
that no matter what, we're blind.
The sinfulness that's surrounds us
covers up, THE LIGHT!

Your demons control you!
They let you know your failure!
They let you know your faults!

Hate

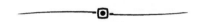

Depression and pain
Stitched to my name
Tears falling like rain
Thoughts shrouded in shame
Emotions shackled and chained
Mentally I've been slain

Who

Who in this world will come save me
I'm battered and broken, but lately
My heart's been screaming and aching
It's calling for someone to save me
The only part left not full of the hatred
My mind and body betray me
Showing me things to cause self-hatred
They lock me in myself, they contain me
To keep me from thriving, they chain me
I need someone!
I need something!
Please save me!

Save Me

I see my soul in the sky
It's screaming "Save me!"

My emotions are in control,
And now they hurt me.

There's nothing left in my mind
I made it empty

To hide myself from the hate
I caused myself, see?

See the pain I made for myself
Ow! I'm scarred deeply.

See all the tears I cried, raining,
They left me thirsty.

Thirsty for her love to feel safety,
Thirsty for her to come and save me!

Morning

Saturday morning,
woke up rain pouring down.

Saturday morning,
woke up and you're not around.

I woke up in pain.
tears on my face,
now I call that rain.

I'm dying of pain.
hole in my chest,
'cause you ran away.

But I am to blame.
I'm lost in myself,
and our love, it was strained.

Woke up this morning.
Rain? It's still pouring.
My mind? It's still hurting.
My heart? It's still yearning.
'Cause you're not around.

Memory

Memory,
falling so tenderly,
drifting away from me.

Memory,
why do you fade from me?
Why do you fall away,
and break away
from time?

Oh memory,
why are you breaking me?
Why do you pull on me,
and tear me
from the heart?

Please memory!
Stop fading away from me!
I need you to stay with me!
So I can feel the way I felt before the fall...

PART 2

DEATH

Addiction

A monkey on your back
There till your light goes black
It needs its fix
To cure the itch

Doubt and **D**epression plant the seed
Feeding it is your deed
It needs its fix
Cure the itch?

It consumes the soul
From the inside it controls
It needs its fix
Cure the itch.

Curing the stress for the moment
But coming back even more potent
It needs its fix
Cure the itch!

Transmitting in your mind like a cancer
An eternal tango and it's the lead dancer
It needs its fix
CURE THE ITCH!

IT NEEDS ITS FIX
CURE THE ITCH!

Overtaken, it has control
Over body, mind, and soul

No more fix
'Cause YOU cure the itch

Violence

(You're)-
—Victim of the hate
—Indicted, it's too late
—Objected to an escape
—Lies; masks for use
—Enslaving loved ones, let them lose!
—Neglect, abuse, and rape
—Convicted at the gate
—Evidence of the hate
What are you?

Depression

Detained
Enchained
Pained
Restrained
Engrained
Strained
Stained
Insane
Obtained
Novocaine

Suicide

————◉————

Sad, but you didn't have to leave.
Unhappy, but loved.
Innocent, but fear took control.
Confining in yourself, never looking for help.
Ironic if you think the pain you bore is gone.
Down the rabbit hole with no way back.
Ending the pain for yourself but for no one else.

PART 3

REBIRTH

Life, is it Important?

Life, is it important?

Death, it keeps encroaching
I, feel like an orphan
Lost, in a big ocean
Cries, filling the voidness
Tears, crawling on my skin
I'm trying to call Him
Pain, I'm growing accustomed
Love, feeling so far gone

Life, is it important?

Hate, filling my bones still
Mind, riddled with holes still
Soul, torn into two still

Life, is it important?

He, may never answer
Time, thinning my ends near
Depression, torture, and anguish
They, spread like a cancer
Thoughts, trap me I'm shackled
Praise, prayer, and confession
They, call Him nearer
I'll wait till I hear Him

Life, is it important?

He, cured me
He, answered
Truth, He gave me

Life, is it important?

King of the Dead

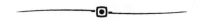

The beast inside,
no longer hides.
It wants to play with me.

King of the Dead,
lost in revenge.
Watching my death again.

Lost in my mind,
set in rewind.
Running away from him.

Lost in a maze,
shackled and chained.
My thoughts entangle me.

Depression…death…
That's all that's said.
Is it too late for me?

Worlds set ablaze,
my thoughts decay.
Tearing my soul in two.

My soul to keep!
Before I sleep!
I pray He shelters me!

Breaks through my skin!
Cures me of sin!
And sets me free again!

Through pain and love,
He rules above,
Slaying the King of Death!

Freedom

Awake with no feeling,
your thoughts, all so misleading.
"Are you dreaming?"

No, this is real,
but you've become so numb
you can no longer feel.

What other outcome
is there when you fall
blindly into his arms.

When you give into all
his anger, that harms
so many others.

You need to come out
from under the covers,
and rid yourself of all doubt.

You must clear your mind,
so the righteous one may enter,
And you will no longer be blind

For he banished your tormentor.
He lifted you of all burdens.
All for your love, it is his guerdon.

...Hope

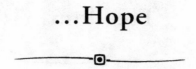

Couldn't see I was blind
Darkness covered my mind

I was chosen I'm the one
Rising up from ash and dust
I spread my wings and break the rust

Set Me Free

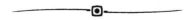

I hope it's not too late for me
for I know I live sinfully.
My demons they have shackled me,
locked me up and lost the key.
Knowing nothing else will set me free

Maybe?
…
Can She?
…
Will She?
…
I'll have to wait and see

So before I close my eyes in peace
I pray that She will shelter me
That all the hate I've kept with me
Will wash away and set me free
So finally when I go to sleep
I'll no longer have to count the sheep

1…2…3…
Laying, covered by my sheets
Hiding from what hides beneath
Hoping She will rescue me
Waiting here patiently
Not knowing if She sees
The pain that I hide…beneath

Bliss

A feather drifting in the wind.
Distant, like a memory.
Vibrant, like an emotion.

A feather drifting in the wind.
Falling, like the setting sun.
Calling, like a mother's love.

A feather drifting in the wind.
Grab it, hold it, keep it near.
So close, there's no longer fear.

A feather drifting in the wind.
Care! Don't let it touch the ground.
Shh! Don't let it make a sound.

A feather drifting in the wind.

His Love

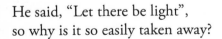

He said, "Let there be light",
so why is it so easily taken away?

See He didn't just give us brightness
to light up the shadows.
No, He rid our world of the Darkness,
the despair, the hate, the anger,
and the demons that feed on fear.
And if you believe that
He too, will light your path.
He heals the sick, and strengthens the weak.
He forgives all who have sinned,
and bathes those who believe
in the riches of His love

Daylight

Dark night,
black sky,
in the moonlight.

                                    Outside,
                                    daylight,
                              with the blue sky.

Last night,
the wind blew and the rain fell.

                                    New day,
                        a blue sky and a rainbow,

Star light,

                                    Daylight,
                  a hopeful sight.

Her Love

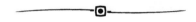

Tears on my face.
My emotions, fighting to win the race.
I can't contain them, I need an escape,
to free myself, and feel her grace.

Running these thoughts through my mind,
to hide myself deep inside.
So no one knows, so no one sees,
the hate and pain that I conceived.

But she has seen, and she believes,
that we could live our lives happily,
Together,
Forever.

Her love's my key.
To unlock my heart,
to set me free.

What If?

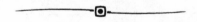

Building blocks,
or rocks,
or sticks,
or stones.
Building ways to get me to your soul.

Find your heart, and tie a bow around.
I just want to show you how WE sounds.

I…
Just don't know how to say it.

What if,
WE could be
the ones to be
together?

What if,
YOU and I
could be the ones
forever?

YOU and I together?
Happiness forever?
Truly we could never?
Hoping we can treasure,
the time we spend together!
For our love could never be measured!

YOU
AND I
TOGETHER...
FOREVER!

Love me

I need your love!
To save me from the corruption
I brought on to myself!

Baby,
Some day you will save me,
and I will thank you greatly
for slaying my demons.

Baby,
One day we'll be happy,
cause you will bring me safety.
Please just wait patiently

Maybe,
When we are both happy
I can see you laughing,
and it will bring a smile to my face.

Maybe,
You were sent to save me.
You light my world up brightly,
'cause baby you are heavenly.

Sorry,
That you have to love me
'Cause my demons are crazy
But baby I will love you too.

Sorry,
That you have to love me,
but baby I promise,
promise to give you that word.

Patience,
You'll have to be patient
I'm sorry for the waiting,
but soon I'll be okay.

She Loves ME!

―――――◉―――――

She saw my soul,
She heard It's cry.
She came to save me.

Not knowing how,
that what she found,
hid something scary.

But when she learned
she did not turn,
instead she said she…

Loved me.

I said it back,
heart turned from black,
now warm and bright, yes.

She set me free,
she had the key
to unlock the chest.

I made myself,
that locked me up.
My love is hers till…

I rest…

Unbrushed Hair

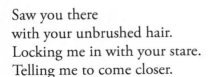

Saw you there
with your unbrushed hair.
Locking me in with your stare.
Telling me to come closer.

Woke up to
my body lying next to you.
Warm, soft, comfortable
hearing, "I LOVE YOU!"

It's crazy
with what we've been through,
but baby
I know I love you.
And lately
my life's been see through.
But baby
you make it visual.

And I know
one day
we will
both grow
old.
And I hope
that I'll…

See you there
with your unbrushed hair.
Sitting with me in our rocking chairs.
Remembering the love we shared.

Lifted

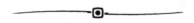

I'm lifted from,
my sins to come.
She saved me and I thanked her.

She set me free,
and now I see
the pain and hate that left me burned!

She saw my light!
Heard screams at night!
No sleep just fright, till she calmed the fear!

Memories

Memories,
distant memories.
Aging so beautifully
Fading so gracefully.
Renewing so rapidly.

But where do they go,
floating all alone?
Somewhere unknown,
a place where no one goes
untapped, untouched.

Brought back
with a smell attached.
Emotions flow,
a nostalgic glow.
Tears or smiles? Unknown

Then gone again,
lost in the wind.
Replaced so fast,
but they will be back.
Memories

THE EXPLANATION

THE THREE STAGES

Decay

Have you ever seen
a grown man falling to his knees?
Yelling,
begging,
pleading,
screaming,
at himself,
because the thing he feared the most was himself?
No?
Seeing him
lying in a field
motionless, unhealed,
filled with fear.
You never knew?
There were so many times
he thought, "I wanna die!"
but all he did was sit in his room and cry.
He was hurt, he was broken!
Depression found him and broke in.
Braking, taking, and defacing
all his feelings.
He was aching,
he didn't want to tell you,
he doesn't know how to tell you,
staring at the mirror
trying to tell himself.

Death

Darkness has a breath!
Lifeless, yeah it's death!
Hoping for a new dawn,
and a new soul to vanquish

Deep inside me
There's a demon screaming
Yelling and telling me to set him free
A new day begins
As the darkness sets in
There's no going back
Once you let your demons attack

Anger and pain,
as you scream out in vain

Lost all control
in a shadow of your own

No one can hear you
no one will know

That the demon in you
has all the control

Rebirth

Birthed through fire
stronger, with new desire.
A new beginning,
a new being.

Memories erased,
pain laid to waste.
A war torn mind,
but hope still shines.

The Phoenix, it flies!
Blazing the sky
purging the world of sin.
Helping the one called, HIM.

A life so divine,
newly revived,
and healed by
pain, hate, and love.

He knows all of them,
without one they die,
but when one has more shine
it tears at you.

Have balance in three,
and someone will set you free!
The Phoenix Trinity.

EPILOGUE

NEW
THOUGHTS

A New Dawn

Emotions…
can easily gain control
because if you fight them
they'll let go.

STRIPPING your mind,
creating a void inside,
and if you aren't careful…
You'll lose yourself along the ride.

But!
Embarrassing lose emotions,
and learning how to cope
will make…

Those sad days a little sadder?
                              yes…
Those bad days a little badder?
                              Yes, but…
Those good days a little better!

Those days are the ones you hold on to!
Those days you never forget!
Those days make the other days worth going through!
Thoses days make life worth living!

Those days are the days you pray for!

Glory

Glory be, to those who give you…

LOVE!
CARE!
SUPPORT!
AFFECTION!
RESPECT!
FRIENDSHIP!
TRUST!

Love takes time to set in,
but stays if it's meant to be.

Care is easy to give,
but is easily overlooked.

Support, if given,
is received 10 fold.

Affection can be misused,
but don't be afraid to give it.

Respect comes in many forms,
you just have to know what to look for.

Friendship is necessary,
but don't let the fake ones in.

Trust is so easy to lose,
but can be earned back with time.

Allow yourself to give theses gifts,
and be grateful when they are given!
Don't let yourself go your whole life
without sharing these gifts with the
people you care about!
But,
be careful who you chose,
because they can break your heart!
But,
when you find the right ones
It'll...
give you life!